Complex numbers

Unit guide

The School Mathematics Project

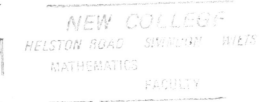

CAMBRIDGE
UNIVERSITY PRESS

Main authors	Stan Dolan
	Ron Haydock
	Barrie Hunt
	Lorna Lyons
	Peter Price
	Paul Roder
	Kevin Williamson
Team Leader	Barrie Hunt
Project director	Stan Dolan

The authors would like to give special thanks to Ann White for her help in preparing this book for publication.

Published by the Press Syndicate of the University of Cambridge
The Pitt Building, Trumpington Street, Cambridge CB2 1RP
40 West 20th Street, New York, NY 10011-4211, USA
10 Stamford Road, Oakleigh, Melbourne 3166, Australia

First published 1991
Reprinted 1994

Produced by Laserwords and 16-19 Mathematics, Southampton

Printed in Great Britain by Scotprint Ltd., Musselburgh.

ISBN 0 521 42663 4

Contents

Introduction to the unit
(for the teacher)

The early chapters of *Complex numbers* are largely independent of any other 16-19 Mathematics units, though it would be advantageous to have studied some sections of *Foundations* and *Mathematical Structure*. Chapter 1 assumes a familiarity with simple vector addition. Chapter 2 involves the algebra associated with polynomial equations, in particular the quadratic formula and the factor theorem. Simple set notation and terms such as associativity and commutativity are used. Chapter 3 assumes a familiarity with composition of functions and with the trigonometric ratios of angles greater than 90°; these are covered in the unit *Functions*. Chapter 4, 5 and 6 are more demanding of both knowledge and mathematical maturity. A prior study of the exponential function, trigonometric identities and series expansions from *Functions*, *Mathematical methods* and *Calculus methods* is needed.

It is recognised that many students working through this unit may be doing so without the benefit of substantial contact time with a teacher. The unit has therefore been written to facilitate 'supported self-study'. It is assumed that even a minimal allocation of teacher time will allow contact at the start and end of each chapter and so

- solutions to all thinking points and exercises are in the students' text;

- a substantial discussion point in one of the opening sections enables the teacher to introduce each chapter;

- a special tutorial sheet can be used to focus discussion at a final tutorial on the work of the chapter.

Chapters 3, 4 and 5 require the use of software to perform complex mappings. The 16-19 Mathematics software, *Exploring complex numbers*, contains a suitable program. Additional short programs written both for the *fx 7000G* and in BBC BASIC are given in the student's text. The software package *Exploring complex numbers* also contains programs needed in Chapter 6 for generating Julia and Mandelbrot sets.

Exploring complex numbers software can be obtained from:

> Franchise Publications
> 3 Wessex House
> Wincombe Lane
> Shaftesbury
> Dorset SP7 8PJ

Some additional notes on the individual chapters my be helpful.

Chapter 1

To establish a visual feel for complex numbers before abstract properties are developed, the unit opens with a geometric approach to complex numbers. The arithmetic operations of the real line are generalised to operations in the complex plane. Vector addition is the model for addition in the complex plane, whilst the expression of complex numbers in polar form leads to a natural definition of multiplication.

Chapter 2

The more conventional algebraic approach to complex numbers via the roots of quadratic equations is followed in this chapter. The complex conjugate and the operation of division are introduced, multiplication is further developed and the chapter closes with de Moivre's theorem.

Chapter 3

Simple loci of the form $|z - z_1| = a$ and $\arg(z - z_1) = k$ are introduced and, in preparation for the more difficult loci in later chapters, a section on polar graphs is included. Simple transformations such as $z \rightarrow z + a$, $z \rightarrow z^*$ and $z \rightarrow z^n$ and combinations of these are introduced through the use of computer software.

Chapter 4

This chapter studies the definition and properties of the e^z function. The remarkable relationship $e^z = \cos z + j \sin z$ is explained and the complex functions $\sin z$, $\cos z$ and $\ln z$ are examined. The work of the chapter shows that trigonometric functions are simple combinations of expononential functions. Functions which seem so different as functions of real variables are therefore seen to be essentially the same.

Chapter 5

An exploration of the concept of inversion and the mapping $z \rightarrow \frac{1}{z}$ leads into the general bilinear mapping $z \rightarrow \frac{az+b}{cz+d}$. The chapter ends by investigating the properties of the Joukowski transformation $z \rightarrow z + \frac{1}{z}$.

Chapter 6

The final chapter of the unit provides a relatively elementary introduction to a current research area of considerable interest; quadratic dynamical systems, including Julia and Mandelbrot sets.

Tasksheets

1 Complex number geometry

1.1 Extending the number system

(a) For the numbers z_1 and z_2 shown in the Argand diagram above, how would you define $z_1 + z_2$? Make sure that your definition is consistent with that for the addition of real numbers.

(b) If 1 is to be the identity element for multiplication, then $1 \times z_1 = z_1$. Describe the geometrical effect of multiplying by z_1. If z_1 is on the real number line, make sure that the effect is consistent with that for real number multiplication.

(c) What properties would you want this new arithmetic of complex numbers to have?

(d) What reasons are there for wanting to extend the real number line?

(a) A vectorial addition would be as shown:

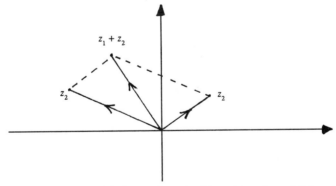

It is easy to see that this is **consistent** with real number addition, i.e. that if z_1 and z_2 were on the real axis then $z_1 + z_2$ would be in the correct position.

(b)

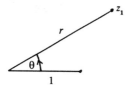

The effect appears to be that of an enlargement, centre the origin and scale factor r, followed by a rotation through angle θ.

This is consistent with the rules for multiplication by positive and negative real numbers.

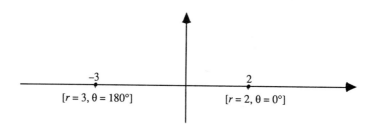

(c) The most important property is that of consistency with the arithmetic of real numbers, which was considered in (a) and (b). The set of complex numbers, $\mathbb{C}$, contains the real numbers, $\mathbb{R}$, as a subset and so results such as $3 \times (-1) = -3$ and $3 + (-1) = 2$ must still be true for the complex numbers 3 and -1.

Properties such as the following would be required to hold:

$1 \times z = z \times 1 = z$ Identity law

$z + \omega = \omega + z$
$z \times \omega = \omega \times z$ }   Commutative laws

$(z + \omega) + t = z + (\omega + t)$
$(z \times \omega) \times t = z \times (\omega \times t)$ }   Associative laws

$z \times (\omega + t) = z \times \omega + z \times t$ Distributive law

It can be shown that these laws do in fact hold for complex numbers and so you can perform the types of operations you are familiar with from real number arithmetic. For example, you are able to multiply out brackets.

(d) Before the introduction of negative numbers, an equation such as $x + 3 = 2$ was simply impossible to solve.

Rational numbers allow you to solve equations such as $3x = 7$ but an equation such as $x^2 = 2$ cannot be solved without the introduction of irrational real numbers.

You have already met simple quadratic equations which cannot be solved using real numbers, for example, $x^2 + x + 1 = 0$ and $x^2 = -1$. As you will see, such equations **can** be solved using complex numbers. You might wonder if this process goes on for ever; other polynomial equations necessitating the extension of the complex numbers to some further number system. The remarkable fact that this does not happen is considered in Chapter 2. The complex numbers are **complete** in the sense that all polynomial equations can be completely solved using complex numbers.

This completeness of the complex numbers gives them a special importance in mathematics and means that considering complex numbers can have a significant unifying effect.

One surprising example of this is considered in Chapter 4 where exponential and trigonometric functions will be seen as special cases of a single complex number mapping.

Exploring polar form

1. $[1, 180°] \times [1, 180°] = [1, 360°] = [1, 0°]$

2. Multiplication is performed by multiplying the moduli and adding the arguments.

    (a) $[2, 30°] \times [3, 60°]$ $= [6, 90°]$

    (b) $[1, 180°] \times [1, 180°]$ $= [1, 360°] = [1, 0°]$

    (c) $[2, -30°] \times [2, 30°]$ $= [4, 0°]$

    (d) $[2, 150°] \times [4, 120°]$ $= [8, 270°] = [8, -90°]$

    (e) $[6, 45°] \times [\frac{1}{6}, -45°]$ $= [1, 0]$

3. $[1, 60°]^2 = [1, 120°]$

    $[1, 60°]^3 = [1, 180°]$

    $[1, 60°]^4 = [1, 240°] = [1, -120°]$

    $[1, 60°]^5 = [1, 300°] = [1, -60°]$

    $[1, 60°]^6 = [1, 360°] = [1, 0°]$

    $[1, 60°]^7 = [1, 420°] = [1, 60°]$

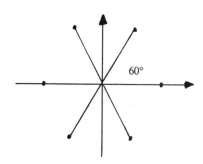

Points representing the powers of $[1, 60°]$ lie on a circle of radius 1, centre 0. Powers above the sixth repeat earlier powers, for example

$$[1, 60°]^7 = [1, 60°]^1, \qquad [1, 60°]^8 = [1, 60°]^2.$$

(continued)

12

4. $[r, \theta]^2 = [r, \theta] \times [r, \theta] = [r^2, 2\theta]$

         $[r, \theta]^3 = [r^3, 3\theta]$

         $[r, \theta]^n = [r^n, n\theta]$

5.   (a) $[r, \theta] \times [\frac{1}{r}, -\theta] = [1, 0]$

        (b)   Since $[1, 0] = 1$, it follows that $\dfrac{1}{[r, \theta]} = [\frac{1}{r}, -\theta]$

        (c)   (i) $[2, 45°] \div [4, 15°] = [2, 45°] \times \dfrac{1}{[4, 15°]} = [2, 45°] \times [\frac{1}{4}, -15°]$

                      $= [\frac{1}{2}, 30°]$

            (ii) $[r, \theta] \div [R, \phi] = [\frac{r}{R}, \theta - \phi]$

6.   (a) $\dfrac{2 \times 10}{5} = 4$

        (b) $50° + 70° - 30° = 90°$

        (c) $2^5 = 32$

7. $z_1 z_2 = [r_1 r_2, \theta_1 + \theta_2]$

        (a) $|z_1 z_2| = r_1 r_2 = |z_1| \, |z_2|$

        (b) $\arg(z_1 z_2) = \theta_1 + \theta_2 = \arg(z_1) + \arg(z_2)$

        (c) $\left|\dfrac{z_1}{z_2}\right| = \dfrac{r_1}{r_2} = \dfrac{|z_1|}{|z_2|}$

        (d) $\arg\left(\dfrac{z_1}{z_2}\right) = \theta_1 - \theta_2 = \arg(z_1) - \arg(z_2)$

Changing forms

1.   (a)   (i) $r = \sqrt{4+25} \approx 5.4$

            (ii) $\alpha = \text{atn}\left(\frac{2}{5}\right) \approx 21.8°$

     (b) $\theta = 180° - \alpha$, $z \approx [5.4 , 158.2°]$

2.   (a) $[\sqrt{2}, -45°]$ (b) $[\sqrt{2}, 135°]$ (c) $[\sqrt{2}, 225°]$ or $[\sqrt{2}, -135°]$

3.   (a) $[\sqrt{13}, 33.7°]$ (b) $[5, 126.9°]$ (c) $[\sqrt{10}, -108.4°]$

4.   (a) $\frac{\sqrt{3}}{2}+\frac{1}{2}j$ (b) $2j$ (c) $-1.5 - 2.6j$

5.   (a)   (i) $[7.81, 50.2°]$ (ii) $[7.81, 129.8°]$ (iii) $[7.81, -129.8°]$

     (b)   (i) $3 + 5.20j$ (ii) $-3 + 5.20j$ (iii) $-3 - 5.20j$

6.   (a) $1 + j = [\sqrt{2}, 45°]$

$$\Rightarrow (1+j)^8 = [\sqrt{2}^{\,8}, 8 \times 45°]$$
$$= [16, 360°]$$
$$= 16$$

     (b) $\frac{\sqrt{3}}{2}+\frac{1}{2}j = [1, 30°]$

$$\Rightarrow \left(\frac{\sqrt{3}}{2}+\frac{1}{2}j\right)^9 = [1, 270°]$$
$$= -j$$

Tutorial sheet

1. (a)

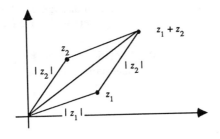

(b)

Since two sides of a triangle are
longer than the third:

$$|z_1 + z_2| \le |z_1| + |z_2|$$

Equality occurs when $\arg(z_1) = \arg(z_2)$

$$|z_1 - z_2| \le |z_1| + |z_2|$$

2. If $z_1 = [r, \theta]$, $z_1^{\,n} = [r, \theta] \times [r, \theta] \times \ldots [r, \theta]$

$$= [r^n, n\,\theta]$$

(a) Then $\quad |z_1^{\,n}| = r^n = |z_1|^n$

(b) Also $\arg(z_1^{\,n}) = n\,\theta = n\arg(z_1)$

3. (a) $(3 + 5j)(-2 + 8j) = -46 + 14j$
    Hence the real part is -46 and the imaginary part is 14.

   (b) $x + jy = 5 - 3j$
   Equating real and imaginary parts, $x = 5$, $y = -3$

4. Subtracting the equations, $\qquad 3\omega = 9 + 15j$

$$\Rightarrow \quad \omega = 3 + 5j$$

$$z = 7 + j$$

(continued)

5.

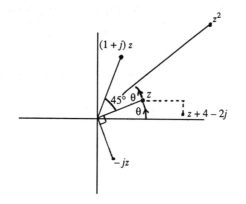

(a) A translation through $\begin{bmatrix} 4 \\ -2 \end{bmatrix}$.

(b) A clockwise rotation through 90°.

(c) A rotation through θ followed by an enlargement with scale factor $|z|$.

(d) A rotation through 45° followed by an enlargement with scale factor $\sqrt{2}$.

6E.   Let $z_1 = x_1 + jy_1$ and $z_2 = x_2 + jy_2$

$$|z_1 + z_2|^2 = |x_1 + x_2 + j(y_1 + y_2)|^2 = (x_1 + x_2)^2 + (y_1 + y_2)^2$$

Similarly $|z_1 - z_2|^2 = (x_1 - x_2)^2 + (y_1 - y_2)^2$

$$|z_1 + z_2|^2 + |z_1 - z_2|^2 = (x_1 + x_2)^2 + (y_1 + y_2)^2 + (x_1 - x_2)^2 + (y_1 - y_2)^2$$
$$= 2x_1^2 + 2x_2^2 + 2y_1^2 + 2y_2^2$$
$$= 2(x_1^2 + y_1^2) + 2(x_2^2 + y_2^2)$$
$$= 2|z_1|^2 + 2|z_2|^2$$

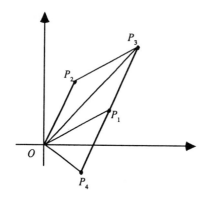

Let P_1 and P_2 represent z_1 and z_2, respectively.

P_3 represents $z_1 + z_2$ and P_4 represents $z_1 - z_2$.

Then $OP_3^2 + OP_4^2 = 2OP_1^2 + 2OP_2^2$

But $OP_2 = \frac{1}{2}P_3P_4$ and so the theorem may be restated as follows:

In any triangle ABC, with median BD,

$$AB^2 + BC^2 = 2BD^2 + \frac{1}{2}AC^2$$

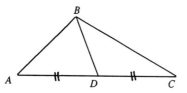

This result is known as Apollonius' median theorem.

2 *Complex number algebra*

2.1   The fundamental theorem of algebra

(a)   Assuming the fundamental theorem, $P_n(z) = 0$ has at least one root in $\mathbb{C}$. Let this be a_1.

   (i)   Explain why there must be a polynomial P_{n-1} of degree $n-1$ such that $P_n(z) = (z - a_1)P_{n-1}(z)$.

   (ii)   Why can you now deduce that
   $P_n(z) = (z - a_1)(z - a_2)P_{n-2}(z)$?

   (iii)   Why does it follow that $P_n(z) = 0$ has precisely n roots ?

(b)   Verify that each of the following equations has precisely two roots.

   (i) $z^2 - 4z + 3 = 0$
   (ii) $z^2 - 4z + 2 = 0$
   (iii) $z^2 - 4z + 5 = 0$

(c)   In what sense does $z^2 - 4z + 4 = 0$ have two roots ?

(d)   Use a graph plotter to help you sketch the graph of
$y = (x + 2)(x^2 - 4x + 5)$.

What conclusions can you make regarding the roots of the equation $z^3 - 2z^2 - 3z + 10 = 0$?

(a)   (i)   If $P_n(a_1) = 0$ then $(z - a_1)$ is a factor of $P_n(z)$ and so you can write
   $P_n(z) = (z - a_1) P_{n-1}(z)$

   (ii)   If $P_{n-1}(z) = 0$ has a root $z = a_2$ then $(z - a_2)$ is a factor of $P_{n-1}(z)$ so
   $P_{n-1}(z) = (z - a_2) P_{n-2}(z)$

   $\Rightarrow P_n(z) = (z - a_1)(z - a_2)\, P_{n-2}(z)$

   (iii)   Similarly

   $P_n(z) = (z - a_1)(z - a_2)(z - a_3)\, P_{n-3}(z)$

   $\vdots$

   $P_n(z) = (z - a_1)(z - a_2)(z - a_3) \dots (z - a_n)\, P_0(z)$ where $P_0(z)$ is a constant.

   Therefore $P_n(z)$ has precisely n roots; $a_1, a_2, \dots, a_n$

(b) (i) $z^2 - 4z + 3 = 0 \Rightarrow (z-1)(z-3) = 0 \Rightarrow z = 1$ or 3

(ii) $z^2 - 4z + 2 = 0 \Rightarrow z = \dfrac{4 \pm \sqrt{8}}{2} \Rightarrow z = 2 \pm \sqrt{2}$

(iii) $z^2 - 4z + 5 = 0 \Rightarrow z = \dfrac{4 \pm \sqrt{-4}}{2} \Rightarrow z = 2 \pm j$

(c) $z^2 - 4z + 4 = 0 \Rightarrow (z-2)(z-2) = 0 \Rightarrow z = 2$

The polynomial has two linear factors and so it is conventional to say that the equation has a repeated root.

(d)

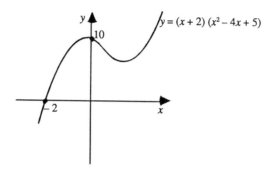

The graph shows that $(x+2)(x^2 - 4x + 5) = 0$ has just one root in $\mathbb{R}$. As a polynomial equation of degree three has precisely three roots, the other two must be complex.

$z^3 - 2z^2 - 3z + 10 = 0 \quad\Rightarrow\quad (z+2)(z^2 - 4z + 5) = 0$

$\Rightarrow\quad z + 2 = 0$ or $z^2 - 4z + 5 = 0$

$\Rightarrow\quad z = -2$ or $z = 2 \pm j$.

18

The quadratic formula

1. (a) $\pm 4j$

    (b) $\pm j \sqrt{5}$

2. $(1 + j)(1 + j) = 1 + 2j + j^2$

    $\qquad\qquad\qquad = 1 + 2j - 1$

    $\qquad\qquad\qquad = 2j$

3. (a) $2j$

    (b) j

    (c) $j - (1 + j) + 1 = 0$

4. $\frac{1}{2}(1 - j)(1 - j) - (1 - j) + 1 \;=\; \frac{1}{2}(1 - 2j + j^2) - 1 + j + 1$

    $\qquad\qquad\qquad\qquad\qquad\qquad = \frac{1}{2}(-2j) + j$

    $\qquad\qquad\qquad\qquad\qquad\qquad = \;\; 0$

5. $\frac{1}{2}x^2 - x + 1 = \frac{1}{2}(x - \alpha)(x - \beta)$ where $\alpha = 1 + j$ and $\beta = 1 - j$

    $\Rightarrow \frac{1}{2}x^2 - x + 1 = \frac{1}{2}(x - 1 - j)(x - 1 + j)$

6. (a) $x = \dfrac{2 \pm \sqrt{4 - 20}}{2}$

    $\qquad = 1 \pm 2j$

    (b) $(1 + 2j)(1 + 2j) - 2(1 + 2j) + 5 = (1 + 4j + 4j^2) - 2 - 4j + 5$

    $\qquad\qquad\qquad\qquad\qquad\qquad\qquad\quad = 1 + 4j - 4 - 2 - 4j + 5$

    $\qquad\qquad\qquad\qquad\qquad\qquad\qquad\quad = 0$

    (c) $x^2 - 2x + 5 = (x - 1 - 2j)(x - 1 + 2j)$

Cardan's method

1. $(u + v)^3 \quad = \quad u^3 + 3u^2v + 3uv^2 + v^3$

    $$= \quad u^3 + v^3 + 3uv\,(u + v)$$

2. The expression $(u^3 + v^3) + 3uv(u + v)$

    will equal $\qquad p + q(u + v)$

    if $u^3 + v^3 = p$ and $3uv = q$.

3. $y = (x - u^3)(x - v^3) \quad = \quad x^2 - (u^3 + v^3)x + u^3v^3$

    $$= \quad x^2 - px + \left(\frac{q}{3}\right)^3$$

    as $u^3 + v^3 = p$ and $uv = \frac{q}{3}$

4. (a) If $x^3 = 9 + 6x$ then $x = u + v$ when u^3 and v^3 are the roots of

    $$x^2 - 9x + \left(\frac{6}{3}\right)^3 = 0 \quad \text{i.e. } x^2 - 9x + 8 = 0$$

    u^3 and v^3 are $\dfrac{9 \pm \sqrt{49}}{2}$

    $\Rightarrow u^3 = 8$ and $v^3 = 1$

    $\Rightarrow u = 2$ and $v = 1$

    $\Rightarrow u + v = 3$

    so if $x^3 = 9 + 6x$ then $x = 3$

    (b) If $x^3 = 12 + 9x$ then $x = u + v$ when u^3 and v^3 are the roots of

    $$x^2 - 12x + \left(\frac{9}{3}\right)^3 = 0$$

    $x^2 - 12x + 27 = 0 \quad \Rightarrow \quad x = 9 \text{ or } x = 3$

    If $u^3 = 9$ then $u = \sqrt[3]{9}$ and if $v^3 = 3$ then $v = \sqrt[3]{3}$

    so $x = \sqrt[3]{9} + \sqrt[3]{3}$

(continued)

20

5.   (a) $(1 + j)^3 = 1 + 3j + 3j^2 + j^3$

$= 1 + 3j - 3 - j$

$= -2 + 2j.$

Similarly,

$(1 - j)^3 = -2 - 2j.$

(b) $x = u + v$ where

$x^3 = -4 + 6x$

and $(u + v)^3 = u^3 + v^3 + 3uv\,(u + v).$

Then $u^3 + v^3 = -4$ and $uv = 2$ i.e. $u^3v^3 = 8.$

u^3 and v^3 are solutions of $t^2 + 4t + 8 = 0$

i.e. $t = \dfrac{-4 \pm \sqrt{-16}}{2} = -2 \pm 2j$

From (a), the equations are solved by

$u = 1 + j$ and $v = 1 - j$

Then $x = u + v = 2.$

It is easy to check that $x = 2$ is a solution of $x^3 = -4 + 6x.$

Note that Cardan's method has resulted in a real solution even though complex numbers were used during the procedure.

Conjugate numbers

1.   (a) $(3 + 4j)\,(3 - 4j) \quad = 9 - 16j^2 \ = 25$

        (b) $(3 + 4j) + (3 - 4j) \ = 6$

        (c) $(x - z)\,(x - z^*) \qquad = x^2 - (z + z^*)x + zz^*$

                           $= x^2 - 6x + 25$

2.   (a) $zz^* \quad = (a + bj)\,(a - bj) \qquad = a^2 - b^2j^2 \ = a^2 + b^2$

        (b) $z + z^* \ = (a + bj) + (a - bj) \quad = 2a$

3. $(2 - 4j)\,(3 + 6j) \ = 30$ is an example when z_1 and z_2 are **not** a conjugate pair. Note, however, that z_1 and z_2 are multiples of a conjugate pair. In the example, $z_1 = 2\,(1 - 2j)$ and $z_2 = 3(1 + 2j)$.

4. $(z - 2 - 3j)(z - 2 + 3j)(z - 1) \ = \ (z^2 - 4z + 13)(z - 1) = \ z^3 - 5z^2 + 17z - 13$

5. $(z^2 + 1)\ (z^2 + 2z + 2) \ = \ 0 \qquad\qquad z = \pm\, j\,, \quad z = -1 \pm j$

6.   (a) $f\,(2) \quad = 24 + 8j$
               $f\,(-2) \ = 0$
               $f\,(j) \quad = 0$
               $f\,(-j) \quad = 4 - 2j$
               $f\,(2j) \quad = -8 - 8j$
               $f\,(-2j) \ = 0$

        (b)   The roots are $-2, j$ and $-2j$.

7.   (a) $(z - 2)(z - 3 - j)(z - 3 + j) = \ 0$

               $(z - 2)(z^2 - 6z + 10) = 0$

               $z^3 - 8z^2 + 22z - 20 \ = \ 0$

        (b) $z^2 + (j - 6)z + (14 - 8j\,) = 0$

        (c) $z^4 - 10z^3 + 33z^2 - 46z + 30 = 0$

        (d) $z^3 - (5 + j)\,z^2 + (2j - 2)\,z + 24 + 8j = 0$

1. (a) $2 + 2j = [2\sqrt{2}, 45°]$

    (b) (i) $(2 + 2j)^6 = [2\sqrt{2}, 45°]^6 = [512, 270°] = [512, -90°]$

    (ii) $-512j$

2. (a) $z^6 = [2, 60°]^6 = [64, 0] = 64$

    (b) $\dfrac{1}{z^5} = [2, 60°]^{-5} = [2^{-5}, -300°] = \left[\dfrac{1}{32}, 60°\right] = \dfrac{1}{64}(1 + \sqrt{3j})$

3. (a) 45° is **one** possible answer.

    (b) Any complex number with arg $(z) = 45n°$, $n \in \mathbb{Z}$, and modulus 1.

    (c) $z^8 = 1 \Rightarrow [r^8, 8\theta°] = [1, 0]$

        (i) The solutions are $[1, 0]$, $[1, 45°]$, $[1, 90°]$, $[1,135°]$, $[1, 180°]$, $[1, -135°]$, $[1, -90°]$, $[1, -45°]$

        (ii) $1 + 0j$, $\dfrac{1}{\sqrt{2}} + \dfrac{1}{\sqrt{2}}j$, $0 + j$, $-\dfrac{1}{\sqrt{2}} + \dfrac{1}{\sqrt{2}}j$, $-1 + 0j$,

        $-\dfrac{1}{\sqrt{2}} - \dfrac{1}{\sqrt{2}}j$, $0 - j$, $\dfrac{1}{\sqrt{2}} - \dfrac{1}{\sqrt{2}}j$

        Note that the roots occur in conjugate pairs.

4. (a) $z^2 = 1 \Rightarrow z = \pm 1$

    (b) $z^3 = 1 \Rightarrow z^3 = [1, 3\theta°] = [1, 360°]$, $z = [1, 0], [1, 120°], [1, -120°]$

    (c) $z^5 = 1 \Rightarrow z^5 = [1, 5\theta°] = [1, 360°]$

        $z = [1, 0], [1, 72°], [1, 144°], [1, -72°] [1, -144°]$

The distributive law

1. The points representing 0, z_1, z_2 and $z_1 + z_2$ form a parallelogram. The images under an enlargement centre O, scale factor r, will still form a parallelogram. The new points are 0, rz_1, rz_2 and $r(z_1 + z_2)$ and so $r(z_1 + z_2) = rz_1 + rz_2$ i.e. $Q = P'$.

2. The origin, the points rz_1 and rz_2, and the point Q form a parallelogram. The origin, the points z_3z_1 and z_3z_2, and the point Q' form another parallelogram.

   As rz_1 is mapped onto z_3z_1 and rz_2 is mapped onto z_3z_2 by the same rotation of $\theta°$ about the origin, it follows that the two parallelograms are congruent. Therefore Q is mapped onto Q' by a rotation of $\theta°$.

3. P' is mapped onto P'' by a rotation of $\theta°$ about the origin and Q is mapped onto Q' by a rotation of $\theta°$ about the origin. As $P' = Q$, it follows that $Q' = P''$.

4.

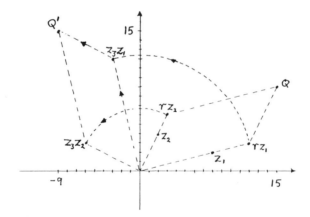

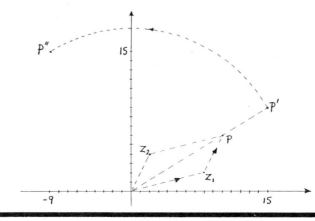

24

Tutorial sheet

1. $z^2 - 2jz + 1 - 0$

    $z = \dfrac{2j \pm \sqrt{4j^2 - 4}}{2}$

    $z = j \pm \sqrt{-2}$

    $z = j\,(1 \pm \sqrt{2})$

2. $z^3 - 5z^2 + 7z + 13 = 0$

    $3 + 2j$ is also a root, giving a quadratic factor of $z^2 - 6z + 13$

    $z^3 - 5z^2 + 7z + 13 = (z^2 - 6z + 13)\,(z + 1) = 0$

    The roots are $3 \pm 2j$, $- 1$

3. If $z = a + jb$ and $\omega = c + jd$, then $z\,\omega = (ac - bd) + j\,(ad + bc\,)$

    $(z\,\omega)^* = (ac - bd\,) - j\,(ad + bc\,)$

    $\qquad = (a - jb\,)\,(c - jd\,)$

    $\qquad = z * \omega *$

4. If $z = a + jb$, $z * = a - jb$.

    Then $\left| z \right| = \sqrt{a^2 + b^2} = \left| z * \right|$.

5. $z^6 = -2j \quad \Rightarrow \quad [r^6 , 6\theta] = [2, 270°]$

    One solution is $z = [\sqrt[6]{2}, 45°]$; the others are at $60°$ intervals around the circle $\left| z \right| = \sqrt[6]{2}$.

    The solutions are

    $[\sqrt[6]{2}, 45°]$, $[\sqrt[6]{2}, 105°]$, $[\sqrt[6]{2}, 165°]$, $[\sqrt[6]{2}, -135°]$, $[\sqrt[6]{2}, -75°]$, $[\sqrt[6]{2}, -15°]$.

6. $$z^n + 1 = 0$$

    For $z = [r, \theta]$, $\qquad \theta = \dfrac{180}{n} + \left(\dfrac{360}{n}\right)m \quad n, m \in \mathbb{Z}$

    $\qquad\qquad\qquad = \dfrac{180}{n}\,(1 + 2m\,)$

    (a) If n is even, θ cannot be $0°$ or $180°$. There are no real roots.

    (b) If n is odd, θ cannot be $0°$ but $\theta = 180°$ when n divides $1 + 2m$. There is one real root, $z = -1$.

(continued)

7. (a) $\omega = -\frac{1}{2} + \frac{1}{2}\sqrt{3}j$ $\omega^2 = -\frac{1}{2} - \frac{1}{2}\sqrt{3}j$

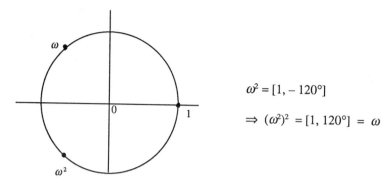

$\omega^2 = [1, -120°]$

$\Rightarrow (\omega^2)^2 = [1, 120°] = \omega$

(b) $z^3 - 1 = (z - 1)(z^2 + z + 1)$

Then $(z - 1)(z^2 + z + 1) = 0$ has roots 1, ω and ω^2

$\Rightarrow \omega = 1$ or $\omega^2 + \omega + 1 = 0$ [Note that $(\omega^2)^2 + (\omega^2) + 1 = \omega + \omega^2 + 1$]

(c) (i) $(1 + \omega)(1 + \omega^2)$ $= 1 + \omega + \omega^2 + \omega^3$
                    $= 0 + 1$
                    $= 1$

(ii) $(1 + \omega^2)^3$ $= 1 + 3\omega^2 + 3\omega^4 + \omega^6$
                    $= 1 + 3\omega^2 + 3\omega + 1$
                    $= 3(1 + \omega + \omega^2) - 1 = -1$

(d) (i) $(z - 2 - \omega)(z - 2 - \omega^2) = 0$
        $(z - 2)^2 - (z - 2)(\omega + \omega^2) + \omega^3 = 0$
        $\Rightarrow (z - 2)^2 - (z - 2)(-1) + 1 = 0$
        $z^2 - 3z + 3 = 0$

(ii) $(z - 3\omega + \omega^2)(z - 3\omega^2 + \omega) = 0$
        $z^2 + (-3\omega^2 + \omega - 3\omega + \omega^2)z + (9\omega^3 - 3\omega^2 - 3\omega^4 + \omega^3) = 0$
        $z^2 + 2z + 13 = 0$

(e) $1 + \omega^n + \omega^{2n} = \begin{cases} 3 & \text{for } n \text{ a multiple of 3 (since } \omega^{3m} = 1) \\ 0 & \text{for all other } n \end{cases}$

8E. $(x - a)^2 + (y - b)^2 = r^2$

$\Rightarrow [x - a + j(y - b)][x - a - j(y - b)] = r^2$ using $X^2 + Y^2 = (X + jY)(X - jY)$
$\Rightarrow [(x + jy) - (a + jb)][(x - jy) - (a - jb)] = r^2$
$\Rightarrow (z - c)(z^* - c^*) = r^2$

3 Loci

3.1 Basic loci

(a) Investigate the set of points $\{z : \arg(z) = \theta\}$ for different values of θ.

(b) If $z = x + jy$, why is $\{z : \arg(z) = 90°\}$ not the same as $\{z : x = 0\}$?

(c) Investigate the set of points $\{z : |z| = c\}$.

(d) If $z = x + jy$ and $|z| = c$, what is the algebraic relationship between x, y and c?

(a)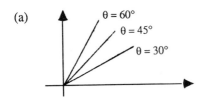

Each set of points is a straight line making an angle θ with the x-axis, since any point on this line satisfies the criterion that $\arg(z) = \theta$. (The origin is excluded from such a set)

(b) $\{z : x = 0\}$ includes the origin and the negative y-axis. At the origin $\arg(z)$ is undefined and on the negative y-axis $\arg(z) = -90°$.

(c)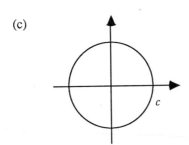

Since $|z|$ is the distance of z from the origin, $\{z : |z| = c\}$ is the set of points which are distance c from the origin i.e. on a circle of radius c.

(d) $\sqrt{x^2 + y^2} = c \Rightarrow x^2 + y^2 = c^2$.

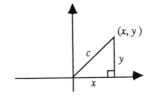

The equation of a circle

1. (a) $x^2 + y^2 = r^2$

    (b) (i) $x - 2$

        (ii) $y - 3$

        $(x - 2)^2 + (y - 3)^2 = r^2$

    (c) $(x - a)^2 + (y - b)^2 = r^2$

2. The centre is at $(4, 2)$.
    The radius is 5.

3.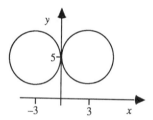

    The centres are at $(-3, 5)$ and $(3, 5)$.

    Therefore the circles have equations $(x + 3)^2 + (y - 5)^2 = 9$

    and $(x - 3)^2 + (y - 5)^2 = 9$

Loci

1. (a) 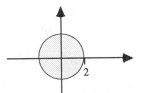   (b)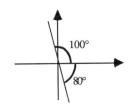

The origin is excluded.

2. (a) (i) 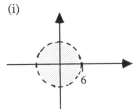   (ii)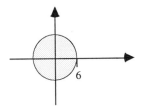

    (b) $|z| < 6$ excludes the boundary of the circle, whilst $x^2 + y^2 \le 36$ includes the boundary. The use of the dotted and solid lines in the diagram above allows you to differentiate between the two cases.

3. (a)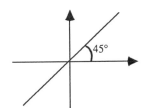

    (b)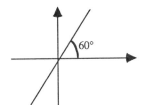

(continued)

(c)

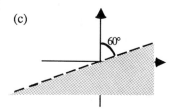

4.   (a)

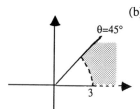

(b)

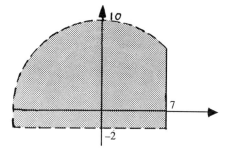

5.   The following are possible ways of describing the sets. There are others.

   (a) $\{z : x \geq 4 \} \cap \{z : y \leq -3 \}$

   (b) $\{z : |z| \leq 6\} \cap \{z : y \geq 0 \}$

   (c) $\{z : |z| > 5\} \cap \{z : -180° \leq \arg (z) \leq - 130° \}$

6.   (a)

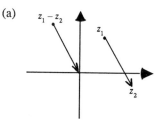

   (b)   The vector from z_1 to z_2 is equal to the vector from $z_1 - z_2$ to the origin. (The vectors are both parallel and equal in length.)

   (c) $|z_1 - z_2|$ is the distance of $z_1 - z_2$ from the origin, and also represents the distance between z_1 and z_2.

   (d) $|z - z_1| = 3$ means 'the distance between z and z_1 is 3'.

(continued)

(e)   (i)

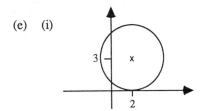

$\{z : |z - z_1| = 3\}$ is the set of points which are distance 3 from z_1
i.e. a circle, centre $2 + 3j$, radius 3.

(ii)

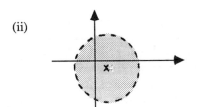

$\{z : |z - z_2| < 5\}$ is the set of points whose distance from z_2 is less than 5
i.e. the interior of a circle, centre $4 - j$, radius 5.

7.   (a)

(b)   For example, $z = 4 + j$, $5 + 2j$, $6 + 3j$ (c)

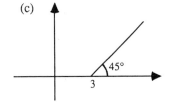

(d)

arg $(z - 2j) = 30°$
arg $z = 30°$

(e)

arg $(z + 4 - j) = 60°$

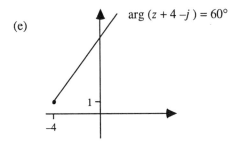

Polar graphs

1.   (a)

θ	0	15	30	45	60	75	90	105	120	135	150	165	180
r	5	4.3	2.5	0	−2.5	−4.3	−5	−4.3	−2.5	0	2.5	4.3	5

θ	195	210	225	240	255	270	285	300	315	330	345	360
r	4.3	2.5	0	−2.5	−4.3	−5	−4.3	−2.5	0	2.5	4.3	5

(b)   The convention is to treat a negative value of r as a reflection of the positive value in the origin. (Some texts adopt the alternative convention that a negative value of r is simply not plotted.)

(c)

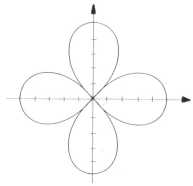

(d)

θ	0	15	30	45	60	75	90	105	etc.
r	0	2.5	4.3	5	4.3	2.5	0	−2.5	

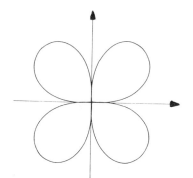

For $90 < θ < 180,$ $r < 0$
           $180 < θ < 270,$ $r > 0$
           $270 < θ < 360,$ $r < 0$

Thus each quadrant is filled with a repeated pattern.

(continued)

2E. $r = 3 \cos 3\theta$ $r = 3 \sin 3\theta$

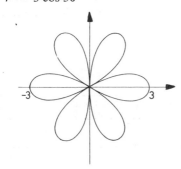

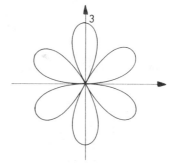

$r = 3 \cos k\,\theta$ has $2k$ petals. $r = 3 \sin k\,\theta$ has $2k$ petals.

3E.   (a)

θ	0	30	45	60	90	120	135	150	180	...
r	4	3.7	3.4	3	2	1	0.6	0.3	0	...

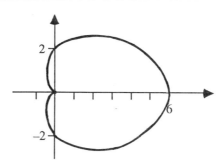

The resulting heart-shaped curve is known as a **cardioid**.

(b) $r = 2\,(1 + 2 \cos \theta)$

θ	0	30	45	60	90	120	135	150	180
r	6	5.5	4.8	4	2	0	−0.8	−1.5	-2

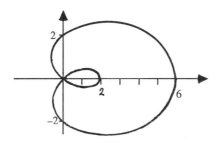

(continued)

Other values of k give similar shaped curves, known as **limacons.** They cross the x-axis when $\theta = 0$, $r = 2\,(1 + k\,)$ and when $\theta = 180°$, $r = -2\,(k-1)$, i.e. at $x = 2\,(k+1)$ and $x = 2(k-1)$.

(c) $r = 2\,(1 - 2 \cos \theta)$

θ	0	30	45	60	90	120	135	150	180
r	-2	-1.5	-0.8	0	2	4	4.8	5.5	6

The resulting graph is the reflection of the graph of $r = 2(1+2 \cos \theta)$ in the y-axis.

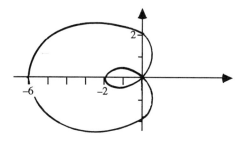

$z \to f(z)$

1.(a)　(i)

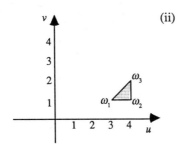

(ii)

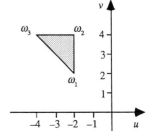

(iii)

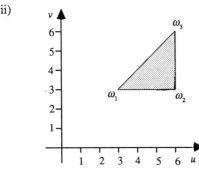

(iv)

(v)

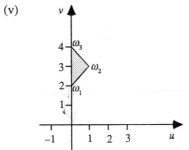

(vi)

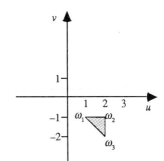

(continued)

(c) (i)   A translation through $\begin{bmatrix} 2 \\ 0 \end{bmatrix}$.

(ii) A translation through $\begin{bmatrix} 1 \\ 1 \end{bmatrix}$.

(iii) An enlargement, scale factor 3, centre the origin.

(iv) An enlargement, scale factor 2, followed by an anti-clockwise rotation through 90° about the origin.

(v) An enlargement, scale factor $|1 + j| = \sqrt{2}$ and an anti-clockwise rotation through arg $(1 + j) = 45°$.

(vi) A reflection in the real axis.

2. (a) $z \rightarrow z + c$ represents a translation through c.

(b) $z \rightarrow c\,z$ represents an enlargement, factor $|c|$ and centre the origin, followed by an anti-clockwise rotation through arg (c).

3. (a) (i)   An enlargement, scale factor 5, centre 0.

(ii) A translation through $-1 + 4j$.

(iii) An anti-clockwise rotation through 90° followed by an enlargement, scale factor 3, centre 0.

(b) (i)   An enlargement, scale factor 5, followed by a translation of $\begin{bmatrix} -1 \\ 4 \end{bmatrix}$.

(ii) A translation of $\begin{bmatrix} -1 \\ 4 \end{bmatrix}$ followed by an enlargement, scale factor 5.

(iii) A reflection in the real axis followed by an enlargement, scale factor 5.

(iv) A reflection in the real axis followed by an anti-clockwise rotation through 90°, and an enlargement, scale factor 3.

(v) A translation through $\begin{bmatrix} -1 \\ 4 \end{bmatrix}$ followed by an anti-clockwise rotation through 90°and an enlargement, scale factor 3.

4. (a) An enlargement, scale factor $|c|$ and centre the origin, followed by an anti-clockwise rotation through arg(c) and a translation through d.

(b) A reflection in the real axis followed by an enlargement, scale factor $|c|$ and centre the origin, and an anti-clockwise rotation through arg (c).

Transformations of loci

1.   (a)   (i)

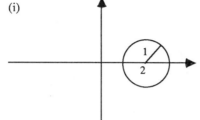

$$\omega = z + 2$$

(ii)

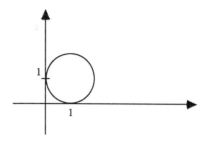

$$\omega = z + 1 + j$$

(iii)

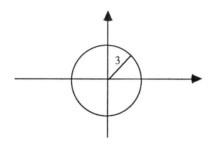

$$\omega = 3z$$

(iv)

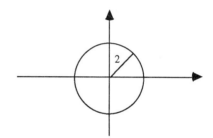

$$\omega = 2j\,z$$

(Note that the circle is invariant under rotation through 90°, although individual points on the circle are not invariant.)

(v)

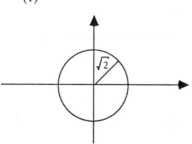

$$\omega = (1 + j)\,z$$

(vi)

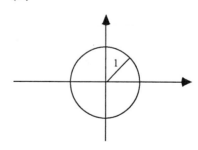

$$\omega = z^{*}$$

(continued)

37

(b) (i) $|\omega - 2| = 1$ (ii) $|\omega - 1 - j| = 1$ (iii) $|\omega| = 3$

(iv) $|\omega| = 2$ (v) $|\omega| = \sqrt{2}$ (vi) $|\omega| = 1$

(c) (i) $z = \omega - 2 \Rightarrow |\omega - 2| = 1$

(ii) $z = \omega - 1 - j \Rightarrow |\omega - 1 - j| = 1$

(iii) $z = \dfrac{\omega}{3} \Rightarrow \left|\dfrac{\omega}{3}\right| = 1 \Rightarrow |\omega| = 3$

(iv) $z = \dfrac{\omega}{2j} \Rightarrow \left|\dfrac{\omega}{2j}\right| = 1 \Rightarrow |\omega| = |2j| \Rightarrow |\omega| = 2$

(v) $z = \dfrac{\omega}{1+j} \Rightarrow \left|\dfrac{\omega}{1+j}\right| = 1 \Rightarrow |\omega| = \sqrt{2}$

(vi) $\omega = z^* \Rightarrow z = \omega^* \Rightarrow |\omega^*| = 1 \Rightarrow |\omega| = 1$

2. (a) (i)   (ii)

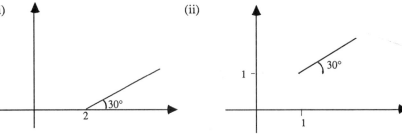

(iii)   (iv)

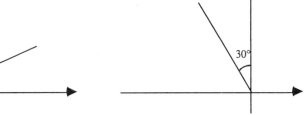

(v)   (vi)

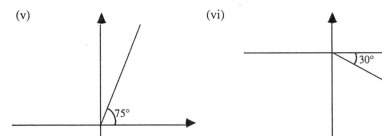

(continued)

38

(b) (i) $\arg(\omega - 2) = 30°$ (ii) $\arg(\omega - 1 - j) = 30°$ (iii) $\arg(\omega) = 30°$

     (iv) $\arg(\omega) = 120°$ (v) $\arg(\omega) = 75°$ (vi) $\arg(\omega) = -30°$

(c) (i) $z = \omega - 2 \Rightarrow \arg(\omega - 2) = 30°$

    (ii) $z = \omega - 1 - j \Rightarrow \arg(\omega - 1 - j) = 30°$

    (iii) $z = \dfrac{\omega}{3} \Rightarrow \arg\left(\dfrac{\omega}{3}\right) = 30° \Rightarrow \arg(\omega) - \arg(3) = 30° \Rightarrow \arg(\omega) = 30°$

     because $\arg(3) = 0$

    (iv) $z = \dfrac{\omega}{2j} \Rightarrow \arg\left(\dfrac{\omega}{2j}\right) = 30° \Rightarrow \arg(\omega) - \arg(2j) = 30°$

                     $\Rightarrow \arg(\omega) - 90° = 30° \Rightarrow \arg(\omega) = 120°$

    (v) $z = \dfrac{\omega}{1+j} \Rightarrow \arg\left(\dfrac{\omega}{1+j}\right) = 30° \Rightarrow \arg(\omega) - \arg(1+j) = 30°$

                      $\Rightarrow \arg(\omega) - 45° = 30° \Rightarrow \arg(\omega) = 75°$

    (vi) $z = \omega^* \Rightarrow \arg(\omega^*) = 30° \Rightarrow \arg(\omega) = -30°$, since $\arg(\omega^*) = -\arg(\omega)$.

3. (a) (i) $z = \omega - 1 - j$. So $\{z : |z + 1 - 3j| \le 4\} = \{\omega : |\omega - 1 - j + 1 - 3j| \le 4\}$

                                           $= \{\omega : |\omega - 4j| \le 4\}$

     (ii) $z = \dfrac{\omega}{2j}$.   So $\{z : |z + 1 - 3j| \le 4\} = \{\omega : |\dfrac{\omega}{2j} + 1 - 3j| \le 4\}$

                                           $= \{\omega : \dfrac{|\omega + 6 + 2j|}{|2j|} \le 4\}$

                                           $= \{\omega : |\omega + 6 + 2j| \le 8\}$

(b)

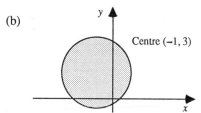

Centre $(-1, 3)$

(i)

Centre $(0, 4)$

(ii)

Centre $(-6, -2)$

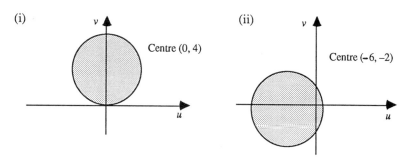

Exploring z^n

1.   (a)

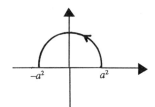

        (b)

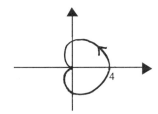

    (c)

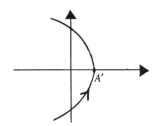

        (d)

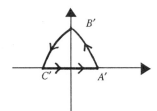

2.   (a)

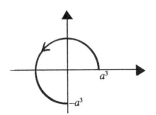

        (b)

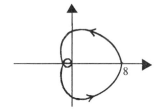

    (c)

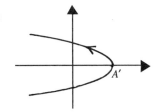

        (d)

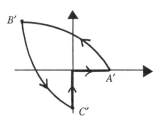

3. $z \to z^2$

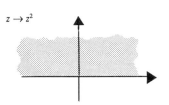

    $z \to z^3$

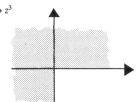

(continued)

40

4. (a) $[r, \theta] \rightarrow [r^2, 2\theta]$

    (b) The distance of the point from 0 changes from r to r^2. If $r > 1$ the distance increases; if $r < 1$ it decreases.

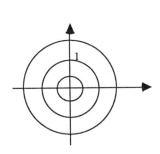

$z \rightarrow z^2$

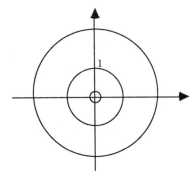

The argument of the point is doubled.

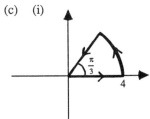

$z \rightarrow z^2$

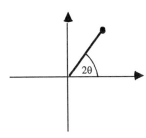

    (c) (i)   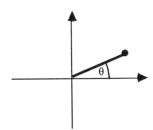   (ii)   (iii)

5. $[r, \theta] \rightarrow [r^3, 3\theta]$.

    (i)      (ii)   (iii)

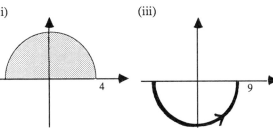

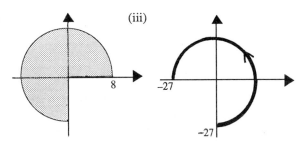

6E.   (a) $|z - a| = a$ is a circle, centre $a + 0j$,
            radius a.

      (b) $r = 2 a \cos \theta$ because the angle in a
            semi-circle is 90°.

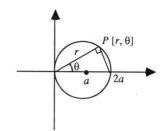

      (c) $R = r^2$, $\varphi = 2\theta$.

            $R = (2a \cos \theta)^2 = 4a^2 \cos^2 \theta = 2a^2 (1 + \cos 2\theta) = 2a^2 (1 + \cos \varphi)$

      (d)   The image is a cardioid.

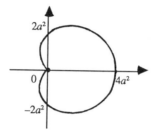

7E.   (a) $u + jv = (x + jy)^2 = (x^2 - y^2) + j (2xy)$

            $\Rightarrow$ $u = x^2 - y^2$ and $v = 2xy$

      (b) $u = a^2 - y^2$ and $v = 2ay$. Eliminating y,

            $u = a^2 - \left(\dfrac{v}{2a}\right)^2$ $\Rightarrow$ $v^2 = 4a^2 (a^2 - u)$.

      (c) $u = x^2 - b^2$ and $v = 2bx$.
            Eliminating x, $v^2 = 4b^2 (u + b^2)$.

      (d)   The curves intersect at $(a^2 - b^2, 2ab)$. At this point, the gradient of
            $v^2 = 4a^2 (a^2 - u)$ is given by

                  $2v \, \dfrac{dv}{du} = -4a^2$

            $\Rightarrow$ $\dfrac{dv}{du} = \dfrac{-4a^2}{4ab} = -\dfrac{a}{b}$

            At the same point, the gradient of $v^2 = 4b^2 (u + b^2)$ is given by

                  $2v \, \dfrac{dv}{du} = 4b^2$

            $\Rightarrow$ $\dfrac{dv}{du} = \dfrac{4b^2}{4ab} = \dfrac{b}{a}$.

            The product of the two gradients is -1 and so the two curves are perpendicular at
            their point of intersection.

(continued)

42

(e)

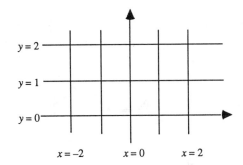

$$x = 0 \quad \rightarrow \quad v = 0$$

$$x = 1 \quad \rightarrow \quad u = 1 - \left(\frac{v}{2}\right)^2$$

$$x = 2 \quad \rightarrow \quad u = 4 - \left(\frac{v}{4}\right)^2$$

$$y = 0 \quad \rightarrow \quad v = 0$$

$$y = 1 \quad \rightarrow \quad u = \left(\frac{v}{2}\right)^2 - 1$$

$$y = 2 \quad \rightarrow \quad u = \left(\frac{v}{4}\right)^2 - 4$$

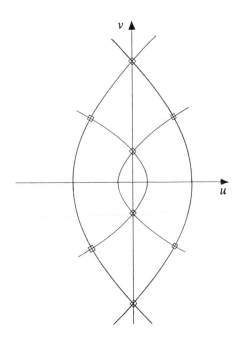

Tutorial sheet

1. (a) 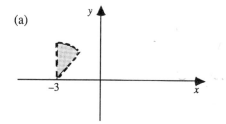   (b)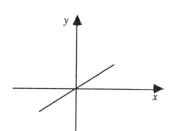

2. (a) $\{\, z : |\, z - 3 - 2j\,| \le 2 \,\} \cap \{\, z : x > 3 \,\}$

    (b) $\{\, z : -120° \ge \arg(z + 2 + 2j) \ge -150° \,\}$

3. (a) $z \to -z\,*$

    (b) $z \to jz\,*$

4. (a) The sequence of transformations is equivalent to a rotation about c.

    (b) $z \to z - 1 - j \to j\,(z - 1 - j) \to j\,(z - 1 - j) + 1 + j = jz + 2$

5. (a)
    $$\left|\, \frac{\omega + 1}{4j} + 4 + 3j \,\right| < 3$$

    $$\Rightarrow \left|\, \omega + 1 + 16j - 12 \,\right| < 3 \,\left|\, 4j \,\right|$$

    $$\Rightarrow \left|\, \omega - 11 + 16j \,\right| < 12$$

    (b) The interior of a circle of radius 12, centre $11 - 16j$.

(continued)

44

6. (a)

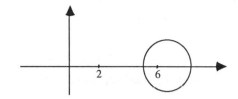

(b) $|x - 2 + jy| = 3|x - 6 + jy|$

$(x - 2)^2 + y^2 = 9((x - 6)^2 + y^2)$

$x^2 + y^2 - 13x + 40 = 0$

$\left(x - \frac{13}{2}\right)^2 = \left(\frac{3}{2}\right)^2$

The circle has radius $\frac{3}{2}$ and centre $\left(\frac{13}{2}, 0\right)$.

7. (a) The distances of z from a and from b add up to k.

(b)

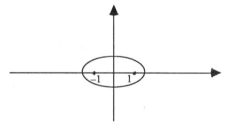

The locus is an ellipse with -1 and 1 as foci.

45

4 The exponential function

4.1 An infinite sequence

(a) Explain how the graph above resembles the graph of S_n for $x = 1$.

(b) Use a program to find the limit of the sequence

$$1, \quad 1 + z, \quad 1 + z + \frac{z^2}{2!}, \quad 1 + z + \frac{z^2}{2!} + \frac{z^3}{3!}, \quad \ldots$$

for

(i) $z = \frac{\pi}{6}j$ (ii) $z = \frac{\pi}{4}j$ (iii) $z = \frac{\pi}{3}j$ (vi) $z = \frac{\pi}{2}j$

What pattern involving trigonometric functions can you spot? If $z = jy$, $y \in \mathbb{R}$, what would you expect to be the value of the limit of the sequence? Check your answer for particular values of y, including $y = 1$.

(c) Because of the usual properties of powers you would expect e^{1+jy} to equal $e \times e^{jy}$. Use a program to find the limit of the sequence for

(i) $z = 1 + \frac{\pi}{6}j$ (ii) $z = 1 + \frac{\pi}{4}j$

(iii) $z = 1 + \frac{\pi}{3}j$ (vi) $z = 1 + \frac{\pi}{2}j$

and comment on your answers.

(d) Suggest a possible definition for e^{x+jy}.

(a) The terms are

$$1$$

$$1 + j$$

$$1 + j - \frac{1}{2} = \frac{1}{2} + j$$

$$\frac{1}{2} + j - \frac{j}{6} = \frac{1}{2} + \frac{5}{6}j$$

$$\frac{1}{2} + \frac{5}{6}j + \frac{1}{24} = \frac{13}{24} + \frac{5}{6}j$$

The sequence converges rapidly, just as in the real case.

The graph differs from that for $x = 1$ in the quarter turns between successive segments. The lengths of corresponding segments in the two graphs are equal.

(b) (i) $\frac{\pi}{6}j$ 0.866025404 + 0.499999999j

(ii) $\frac{\pi}{4}j$ 0.707106782 + 0.707106781j

(iii) $\frac{\pi}{3}j$ 0.500000001 + 0.866025403j

(vi) $\frac{\pi}{2}j$ 0   +   1j

It looks as if the sequence for $z = yj$ always converges to $\cos y + j \sin y$, where y is measured in radians. For example, if $z = j$ then you would expect the sequence to converge to

$\cos 1 + j \sin 1 \approx 0.540302306 + 0.841470985j$.

It is easy to use the program to check that this is indeed the case.

(c) (i) 2.35410112 + 1.35914091j etc.

(ii) 1.92211551 + 1.92211551j

(iii) 1.35914091 + 2.35410112j

(iv) 0   + 2.71828183j

Each number is e times the corresponding number in the answer to (b). For example,

0.866025404 x e ≈ 2.35410112

When $z = 1 + jy$, the limit of the sequence appears to be

$e^1 (\cos y + j \sin y)$.

(d) It appears that the limit of the sequence when $z = x + jy$ is $e^x (\cos y + j \sin y)$. This can therefore be taken as the definition of e^z. Using the definition you can check whether e^z possesses the same algebraic properties as its real counterpart. For example, does $e^{z_1 + z_2} = e^{z_1} \times e^{z_2}$? Such algebraic properties will be considered after the geometric properties of e^z have been investigated using a computer program.

$$z \rightarrow e^z$$

1.   (a)

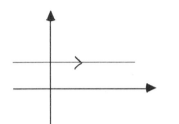 $\rightarrow$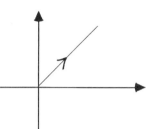

     (b)

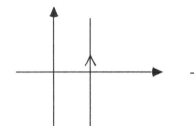 $\rightarrow$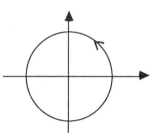

     (c)

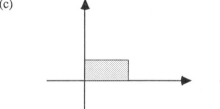 $\rightarrow$

     (d)

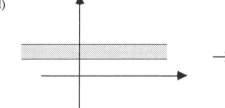 $\rightarrow$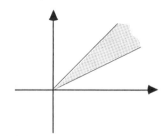

The sector may be in any quadrant(s).

2.   The solution to question 2 is given in the student's text.

(continued)

3. $z = x + jy$ and $\omega = u + jv$

(a) $u + jv = e^{x+jy} = e^x . e^{jy} = e^x (\cos y + j \sin y)$

$\Rightarrow u = e^x \cos y$ and $v = e^x \sin y$

(b) $u = e^a \cos y$ and $v = e^a \sin y$

$\Rightarrow u^2 + v^2 = e^{2a} (\cos^2 y + \sin^2 y) = e^{2a}$

The image is a circle in the ω-plane with radius e^a.

(c) $u = e^x \cos b$ and $v = e^x \sin b$

$\Rightarrow \dfrac{v}{u} = \tan b$

$\Rightarrow v = (\tan b) u$, the equation of a straight line in the ω-plane through the origin.

(d) The images are a circle, centre the origin, and a half line through the origin. These are clearly orthogonal.

A proof can be given using calculus.

For the circle:

$u^2 + v^2 = e^2$

$\Rightarrow 2u + 2v \dfrac{dv}{du} = 0 \Rightarrow \dfrac{dv}{du} = -\dfrac{u}{v}$

For the line:

$v = (\tan 1)u$

$\Rightarrow \dfrac{dv}{du} = \tan 1 = \dfrac{v}{u}.$

At the point of intersection, the product of the gradients is $-\dfrac{u}{v} \times \dfrac{v}{u} = -1$. The images are therefore orthogonal.

49

Complex powers

1.　(a)　$e^{j\frac{\pi}{6}} = \frac{\sqrt{3}}{2} + \frac{1}{2}j$

　　(b)　$e^{-j\frac{\pi}{2}} = -j$

　　(c)　$e^{3j} = \cos 3 + j \sin 3 \approx -0.99 + 0.14j$

　　(d)　$e^{2-3j} = e^2 \cdot e^{-3j} = e^2 (\cos 3 - j \sin 3) \approx -7.32 + 1.04j$

　　(e)　$e^{j\pi} = \cos \pi + j \sin \pi = -1$

2.　(a)　$k = \ln 2$ i.e. $2 = e^{\ln 2}$

　　(b)　$2^j = e^{(\ln 2)j} = \cos (\ln 2) + j \sin (\ln 2) \approx 0.77 + 0.64j$

3.　(a)　$4^{-j} = e^{-(\ln 4)j} \approx 0.18 - 0.98j$

　　(b)　$7^{2-3j} = 49 \cdot e^{(-3 \ln 7)j} \approx 44.2 + 21.1j$

4E.　You would need to go back to the definitions,

$$e^{z_1} = e^{x_1} (\cos y_1 + j \sin y_1) \text{ and } e^{z_2} = e^{x_2} (\cos y_2 + j \sin y_2),$$

and then multiply e^{z_1} and e^{z_2} without assuming any properties of the e^z function.

Then　$e^{z_1} \times e^{z_2} = e^{x_1} \times e^{x_2} \times (\cos y_1 + j \sin y_1) \times (\cos y_2 + j \sin y_2)$

$$= e^{x_1 + x_2} (\cos y_1 \cos y_2 - \sin y_1 \sin y_2 + j (\cos y_1 \sin y_2 + \sin y_1 \cos y_2))$$

$$= e^{x_1 + x_2} (\cos (y_1 + y_2) + j \sin (y_1 + y_2))$$

$$= e^{x_1 + x_2 + j (y_1 + y_2)}$$

$$= e^{z_1 + z_2}$$

Sin z and cos z

1. (a) $e^{jx} = \cos x + j \sin x$

   $e^{-jx} = \cos(-x) + j\sin(-x) = \cos x - j\sin x$

   $\Rightarrow \frac{1}{2}(e^{jx} + e^{-jx}) = \cos x$

   (b) $\sin x = \frac{1}{2j}(e^{jx} - e^{-jx})$

2. (a) $\sin^2 z + \cos^2 z = \frac{1}{4}(e^{2jz} + 2 + e^{-2jz}) - \frac{1}{4}(e^{2jz} - 2 + e^{-2jz}) = 1$

   (b) $\sin t \cos z + \cos t \sin z = \frac{1}{2j}(e^{jt} - e^{-jt})\frac{1}{2}(e^{jz} + e^{-jz}) + \frac{1}{2}(e^{jt} + e^{-jt})\frac{1}{2j}(e^{jz} - e^{-jz})$

   $$= \frac{1}{2j}(e^{j(t+z)} - e^{-j(t+z)})$$

   $$= \sin(t + z)$$

3. (a) $\sin\left(j\frac{\pi}{3}\right) = \frac{1}{2j}(e^{-\frac{\pi}{3}} - e^{\frac{\pi}{3}}) \approx 1.25j$

   (b) $\cos(2 + 3j) = \cos 2 \cos 3j - \sin 2 \sin 3j$

   $$= \frac{1}{2}(e^{-3} + e^3)\cos 2 - \frac{1}{2j}(e^{-3} - e^3)\sin 2$$

   $$\approx -4.19 - 9.11j$$

   (c) $\sin(2 - j) = \sin 2 \cos j - \cos 2 \sin j$

   $$= \frac{1}{2}(e^{-1} + e)\sin 2 - \frac{1}{2j}(e^{-1} - e)\cos 2$$

   $$\approx 1.40 + 0.49j$$

4. (a) $e^{jz} = \frac{1}{2}(e^{jz} + e^{-jz}) + \frac{1}{2}(e^{jz} - e^{-jz})$

   $$= \cos z + j\sin z$$

   (b) Assuming that the expansions of cos x and sin x extend naturally to complex numbers, you would expect

   $$\cos z + j\sin z = (1 - \frac{z^2}{2!} + \frac{z^4}{4!} - \ldots) + j(z - \frac{z^3}{3!} + \frac{z^5}{5!} - \ldots)$$

   $$= 1 + (jz) + \frac{(jz)^2}{2!} + \frac{(jz)^3}{3!} + \frac{(jz)^4}{4!} + \ldots$$

   $$= e^{jz}$$

1. (a) $e^{j\frac{\pi}{4}} = \cos\frac{\pi}{4} + j\sin\frac{\pi}{4} = \frac{1}{\sqrt{2}}(1+j)$

    (b) $3^{2+4j} = 9 \times 3^{4j} = 9 \times e^{4j\ln 3}$

    $= 9\,(\cos(\ln 81) + j\sin(\ln 81))$

    $\approx -2.81 - 8.549j$

    (c) $\cos\left(\frac{\pi}{3} - 2j\right) = \cos\frac{\pi}{3}\cos 2j + \sin\frac{\pi}{3}\sin 2j$

    $\approx 1.88 + 3.14j$

    (d) $\ln(5j) = \ln 3 + j\left(\frac{\pi}{2} + 2n\pi\right),\ n \in \mathbb{Z}.$

2. $\ln(z_1\,z_2) = \ln\left(r_1\,e^{j\theta_1} \times r_2\,e^{j\theta_2}\right) = \ln\left(r_1\,r_2\,e^{j(\theta_1+\theta_2)}\right)$

    $= \ln(r_1\,r_2) + j(\theta_1 + \theta_2) + 2n\pi j$

    $= \ln r_1 + \ln r_2 + j\,\theta_1 + j\,\theta_2 + 2n\pi j$

    $= \ln r_1 + j\,\theta_1 + \ln r_2 + j\,\theta_2 + 2n\pi j$

    $= \ln z_1 + \ln z_2$

3.

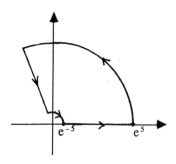

The angle of the sector is 2 radians.

(continued)

52

4. $\frac{1}{2j}(e^{jz}-e^{-jz})=2.$

Let $t=e^{jz}$, then $t^2-4jt-1=0$

$\Rightarrow t=\frac{4j\pm\sqrt{-16+4}}{2}=(2\pm\sqrt{3})j$

$e^{jz}=(2\pm\sqrt{3})j$

$\Rightarrow e^{-y}(\cos x+j\sin x)=(2\pm\sqrt{3})j$

One solution is $x=\frac{\pi}{2}$ and $y=\ln(2+\sqrt{3})$

Then $z=\frac{\pi}{2}+j\ln(2+\sqrt{3})$

5E. (a) $\sin(x+j)=\sin x\cos j+\cos x\ \sin j$

$\cos j=\frac{1}{2}(e^{j^2}+e^{-j^2})=\frac{1}{2}(e^{-1}+e^1)$

$\sin j=\frac{1}{2}(e^{j^2}-e^{-j^2})=j\frac{1}{2}(e^1-e^{-1})$

Then $u=a\sin x$ and $v=b\cos x$

$\left(\frac{u}{a}\right)^2+\left(\frac{v}{b}\right)^2=1$, an ellipse

(b) $\sin(1+jy)=\sin 1\times\cos jy+\cos 1\times\sin jy$

$u=\frac{1}{2}\sin 1\times(e^y+e^{-y})$ and $v=\frac{1}{2}\cos 1\times(e^y-e^{-y})$

$\left(\frac{u}{\sin 1}\right)^2-\left(\frac{v}{\cos 1}\right)^2=1$, a hyperbola.

6E. $j^j=\left(e^{\frac{\pi}{2}j}\right)^j=e^{-\frac{\pi}{2}}$, a real number.

5 *Further transformations*

5.1 Inversion

<blockquote>

(a)   Describe your findings about inversion obtained by using a computer program.

(b)   Transform the equation $|z - a| = \lambda |z - b|$ using $\omega = \dfrac{1}{z}$. Describe the corresponding locus in the ω-plane.

(c)   By considering the cases
$$\lambda = 1, \quad |a| = |b|$$
$$\lambda = 1, \quad |a| \neq |b|$$
$$\lambda \neq 1, \quad |a| = \lambda |b|$$
$$\lambda \neq 1, \quad |a| \neq \lambda |b|$$
deduce the results listed below.

</blockquote>

(a)   A straight line through the origin maps to its mirror image in the x-axis.

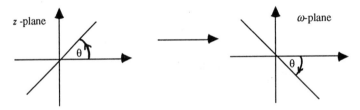

Other straight lines appear to map to circles.

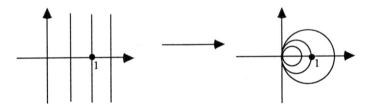

A circle through the origin maps to a straight line. This should have been expected because it simply reverses the transformation of a straight line which does not pass through the origin.

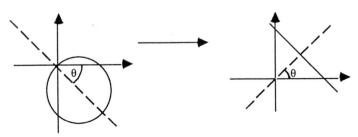

A circle which does not pass through the origin maps to another circle which does not pass through the origin.

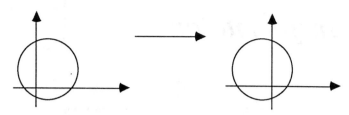

(b)

$$\left|\frac{1}{\omega} - a\right| = \lambda \left|\frac{1}{\omega} - b\right|$$

$$\Rightarrow \left|1 - a\omega\right| = \lambda \left|1 - \omega b\right|$$

$$\Rightarrow \left|\omega - \frac{1}{a}\right| |a| = \lambda \left|\omega - \frac{1}{b}\right| |b|$$

$$\Rightarrow \left|\omega - \frac{1}{a}\right| = \lambda \frac{|b|}{|a|} \left|\omega - \frac{1}{b}\right|$$

This is the locus of
$$\begin{cases} \text{a circle if } \lambda \dfrac{|b|}{|a|} \neq 1 \\[2em] \text{a line if } \lambda \dfrac{|b|}{|a|} = 1 \end{cases}$$

(c)   **$\lambda = 1, |a| = |b|$**

A line which passes through the origin ($z = 0$ satisfies the equation) maps to another line through the origin.

$\lambda = 1, |a| \neq |b|$

A line which does not pass through the origin ($z = 0$ does not satisfy the equation) maps to the circle

$$\left|\omega - \frac{1}{a}\right| = \frac{|b|}{|a|} \left|\omega - \frac{1}{b}\right|$$

$\omega = 0$ satisfies this equation and so the circle passes through the origin.

$\lambda \neq 1, |a| = \lambda |b|$

A circle through the origin maps to a straight line which does not pass through the origin.

$\lambda \neq 1, |a| \neq \lambda |b|$

A circle not through the origin maps to a circle which does not pass through the origin.

Linear transformations

1. (a) $z \rightarrow z + 0.5$ a translation

    $z + 0.5 \rightarrow \dfrac{1}{z + 0.5}$ an inversion

    $\dfrac{1}{z + 0.5} \rightarrow \dfrac{2}{z + 0.5}$ an enlargement

    $\dfrac{2}{z + 0.5} \rightarrow 2 + \dfrac{2}{z + 0.5}$ a translation

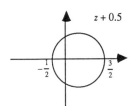 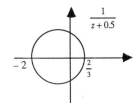 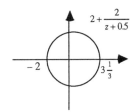

2. $\dfrac{6z - 2}{3z + 1} = \dfrac{2(3z + 1) - 2 - 2}{3z + 1} = 2 + \dfrac{-\dfrac{4}{3}}{z + \dfrac{1}{3}}$

    The transformation can be thought of as a combination of the following sequence of transformations:

    a translation of $\begin{bmatrix} \frac{1}{3} \\ 0 \end{bmatrix}$;

    an inversion;

    an enlargement, centre the origin, scale factor $\dfrac{4}{3}$;

    a rotation of 180° about the origin;

    a translation of $\begin{bmatrix} 2 \\ 0 \end{bmatrix}$.

3. (a) $z \rightarrow z + \gamma$ a translation

    $z + \gamma \rightarrow \dfrac{1}{z + \gamma}$ an inversion

    $\dfrac{1}{z + \gamma} \rightarrow \dfrac{\beta}{z + \gamma}$ an enlargement followed by a rotation
                                                 (a spiral enlargement)

    $\dfrac{\beta}{z + \gamma} \rightarrow \alpha + \dfrac{\beta}{z + \gamma}$ a translation

(continued)

(b) If α and/or γ were real, the corresponding translation would be parallel to the x-axis.

If β were real, then the rotation spiral enlargement would simply be an enlargement or an enlargement and a rotation of 180°.

Essentially, it does not matter whether α, β and γ are real or are not real.

4. 'Circles' map to 'circles' under translations, inversions and spiral enlargements. Any combination of these transformations therefore also maps 'circles' to 'circles'.

5. (a) (i) $2 \to 4$

(ii) $1 + j \to 3 + \dfrac{2}{1+j} \quad = 3 + \dfrac{2(1 - j)}{2}$

$$= 4 - j$$

(iii) $0 \to \infty$

(b) The points 2, $1 + j$ and 0 are all on $|z - 1| = 1$ and so the image passes through 4, $4 + j$ and ∞. The fact that the image of one of these points is infinite means that the image is a straight line.

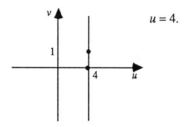

$u = 4.$

1.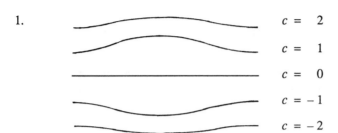

   $c = 2$

   $c = 1$

   $c = 0$

   $c = -1$

   $c = -2$

2. There are many ways of proving this result. Perhaps the most elegant way is as follows:

   $$z + \frac{1}{z} = z + \frac{z^*}{zz^*}$$

   $$= z + z^*, \text{ if } |z| = 1$$

   $$= 2x$$

   So $u = 2x$ and $v = 0$.

3. $$z + \frac{1}{z} = x + jy + \frac{x - jy}{x^2 + y^2}$$

   $$= x + \frac{x}{x^2 + y^2} + j\left(y - \frac{y}{x^2 + y^2} \right)$$

   $$= x + \frac{x}{x^2 + y^2} + jc$$

   So $v = c$.

4. (a) The image is symmetrical about the real axis, though there are several possible shapes. For example:

   a circle centre the origin transforms onto an ellipse;

   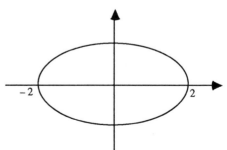

(continued)

a circle passing through − 1 transforms into a curve with a cusp at − 2;

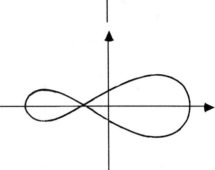

a circle enclosing just one of the points + 1 and − 1 transforms into a double loop.

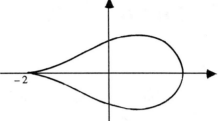

(b)   The image is symmetrical about the imaginary axis. Again there is more than one possible shape:

a circle passing through both − 1 and + 1 transforms into a circular arc;

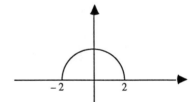

a circle not passing through ± 1 transforms into the shape shown.

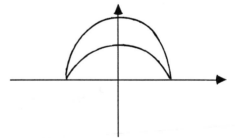

(c)   The resulting shape is called the **Joukowski aerofoil** and resembles the familiar aeroplane wing cross-section.

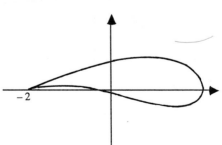

1. The mapping can be broken down into the following sequence of transformations.

    $$z_1 = 2z, \quad z_2 = z_1 + 1, \quad z_3 = \frac{1}{z_2}, \quad z_4 = -9z_3, \quad \omega = 5 + z_4$$

    The effect of these on the line $x = 2$ is illustrated below

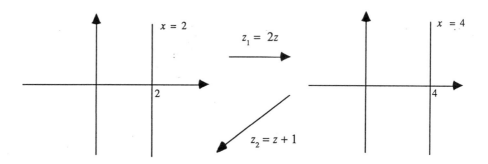

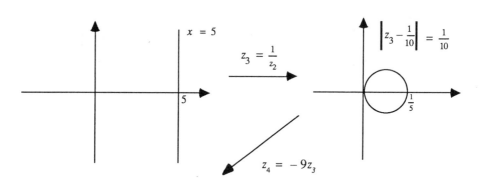

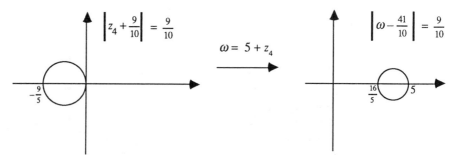

(continued)

2.   (a) ω moves clockwise around the semi-circle $\left|\omega+1\right| = 2$, Im $(\omega) \leq 0$.

    (b) ω moves clockwise around the semi-circle $\left|\omega+\frac{1}{3}\right| = \frac{1}{6}$, Im $(\omega) \geq 0$.

    (c) ω moves away from the origin along the half line $v = \frac{3}{4}$, $u \geq 0$.

    (d) $\omega = -2j + \dfrac{1}{z-j}$

        ω moves clockwise around a major arc of the circle

$$\left|\omega+\frac{7}{3}j\right| = \frac{2}{3}, \text{ from } \frac{1}{5}(2-9j) \text{ to } \frac{1}{5}(-2-9j).$$

3.   If P is the point z, OP has length $\dfrac{c^2}{|z|}$. $\overrightarrow{OP}$ is parallel to z and so $\overrightarrow{OP} = \lambda z$.

$$\text{Then } \lambda|z| = \frac{c^2}{|z|} \Rightarrow \lambda = \frac{c^2}{|z|^2}$$

$$\overrightarrow{OP} = \frac{c^2 z}{|z|^2} = \frac{c^2 z}{zz^*} = \frac{c^2}{z^*}$$

4.   (a) $z + 2 = \dfrac{1}{\omega}$

        $\Rightarrow z = \dfrac{1}{\omega} - 2$

        $\Rightarrow 1 = |z| = \left|\dfrac{1}{\omega} - 2\right|$

    (b) $1 = \left|\dfrac{1-2\omega}{\omega}\right|$

        $|\omega| = \left|1-2\omega\right|$

        $|\omega| = 2\left|\omega-\frac{1}{2}\right|$

        A circle centre $\left(\frac{2}{3}, 0\right)$, radius $\frac{1}{3}$.

5.

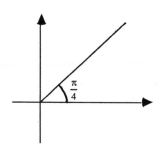

$$\omega = \frac{r}{\sqrt{2}}(1+j) + \frac{1}{\sqrt{2}\,r}(1-j)$$

$$u = \frac{1}{\sqrt{2}}\left(r+\frac{1}{r}\right), \quad v = \frac{1}{\sqrt{2}}\left(r-\frac{1}{r}\right). \text{ Then } u^2 - v^2 = 2.$$

6 *Towards chaos*

6.1   Sequences of complex numbers

> Consider the sequence $\{(1+j)^n\}$. In which other ways could this sequence be defined?
>
> Describe and comment on possible graphical representations of the sequence.

The sequence $\{(1+j)^n\}$ could be defined

- by listing the first few members:

    $$1+j, (1+j)^2, (1+j)^3, \ldots$$

- using a recurrence relation:

    $$z_{n+1} = (1+j)z_n, \quad z_1 = 1+j$$

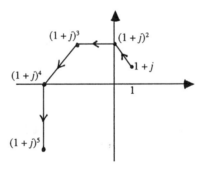

In the step diagram representing the sequence there is a change in direction between successive directed line segments of $\frac{\pi}{4}$, representing the argument increasing by arg $(1+j)$.

The vector representation shown in the text is good for showing the successive increases in argument by $\frac{\pi}{4}$ and also for showing successive multiplications in modulus by a factor of $|1+j| = \sqrt{2}$.

The drawback to the vector and point methods is that the order of the sequence is not shown clearly.

1.   (a)   For the system given by $z_{n+1} = [1, \frac{\pi}{3}] z_n$, all non-zero points are periodic of order 6.

     (b)   For the system given by $z_{n+1} = [1, \frac{\pi}{4}] z_n$, all non-zero points are periodic of order 8.

2.   In the system given by $z_{n+1} = z_n^2$,

     (a)   the points $\left[1, \frac{(2n+1)\pi}{16}\right]$ ($n = -8, -7, \dots, 7$) are periodic of order 6;

     (b)   the points $\left[1, \frac{(2n+1)\pi}{64}\right]$ ($n = -32, -31, \dots, 31$) are periodic of order 8.

Other answers are possible for questions 1 and 2.

3.   (a) $-\frac{1}{2} - \frac{1}{2}j$ is a fixed point. There are no periodic points.

     (b)   There are no fixed or periodic points. The relation $z_{n+1} = z_n + j$ translates all points through j.

     (c) $-1 - \frac{\sqrt{3}}{2} - \frac{1}{2}j$ is a fixed point. All other points are periodic of order 12.

4.   (a)   The orbit generated by $z_0 = 0$ is $0, 1, 1 + j, -1, 1 + j, \dots$
           -1 and $1 + j$ are periodic points of order 2.

     (b)   If z is a fixed point then

$$jz^2 - z + 1 = 0$$
$$\Rightarrow z^2 + jz - j = 0$$

$$\Rightarrow z = \frac{-j \pm \sqrt{-1 + 4j}}{2}$$

$$-1 + 4j = \left[\sqrt{17}, 104.0°\right], \text{ so}$$

$$z = \frac{-j \pm [2.0305, 52.0°]}{2}$$

z is $0.625 + 0.300j$

(continued)

5.   The translation is $z \rightarrow z + \frac{a}{2}$.

Then $\left(z + \frac{a}{2}\right)^2 + c = z^2 + az + b$

$\Rightarrow \quad c = b - \frac{a^2}{4}$.

6E.   (a) $z_{n+1} = z_n \left(z_n + \frac{c}{z_n}\right)$

$\Rightarrow |z_{n+1}| = |z_n| \left|z_n + \frac{c}{z_n}\right|$

$\Rightarrow |z_{n+1}| \geq |z_n| \left(|z_n| - \frac{|c|}{|z_n|}\right)$

Then $|z_{n+1}| \geq |z_n| \left(|z_n| - 1\right)$

Since $|z_n| > 2$, $|z_n| - 1 > 1$ and so $|z_{n+1}| > |z_n|$.

(b)   As in (a), $|z_{n+2}| \geq |z_{n+1}| \left(|z_{n+1}| - 1\right)$.

From (a), $|z_{n+1}| \geq |z_n| \left(|z_n| - 1\right)$ and $|z_{n+1}| - 1 > |z_n| - 1$.

Therefore, $|z_{n+2}| > |z_n| \left(|z_n| - 1\right)\left(|z_n| - 1\right)$.

Repeating this for z_{n+3}, z_{n+4}, ... yields $|z_{n+k}| > |z_n| \left(|z_n| - 1\right)^k$.

Since $|z_n| - 1 > 1$, the moduli of successive terms tend to $+\infty$ and so the sequence diverges to infinity.

(c)   Suppose $|c| > 2$.

For $z_1 = 0$, $z_2 = c$. Then $|z_2| \geq |c|$ and $|z_2| > 2$. By part (b), the iterative sequence diverges and so c is **not** in the Mandelbrot set.